Bathgate

in old picture postcards

GB ISBN 90 288 3167 3

© 1985 European Library – Zaltbommel/The Netherlands

Second edition, 1996: reprint of the original edition of 1985.

Bathgate
in old picture postcards

by William Fyfe Hendrie

European Library ZALTBOMMEL/THE NETHERLANDS

Bathgate's coat of arms showing the castle and the town's Latin motto.

About the author:

After graduating from Edinburgh University, William Fyfe Hendrie, began his career as history master at Bathgate's Lindsay High School. He later became Headmaster of Torphichen Primary School and was then promoted to the position of Head of Murray-field School, Blackburn near Bathgate. He is now Head of Lothian Region's largest primary school, Linlithgow Primary, but still has his home in the village of Torphichen. As well as interesting his pupils in local history, including starting his award winning junior guide scheme at Linlithgow Palace, he has done much to increase adult interest in the history of West Lothian District by lecturing for the extra mural departments of both Edinburgh and Stirling universities and by writing many local history books and advising on several television programmes on the subject. This is his second book in the series 'in old picture postcards', the first being about his home town, Bo'ness, on the River Forth. Most of the postcards and old photographs for this new volume have been supplied by Mrs. Brady of West Lothian District Library and by Mr. James Nicol of Academy Street, whose lantern shows about old Bathgate brighten many a winter evening for organisations in the town.

INTRODUCTION

Bathgate is situated midway between Edinburgh and Glasgow, right in the middle of Central Scotland in what was formerly Linlithgowshire and what since local government re-organisation in the mid-1970's has become the West Lothian District of Lothian Region, for which the town is the administrative centre.

This rise in the importance of Bathgate since re-organisation is somewhat appropriate as local tradition has always maintained that in days gone by the surrounding area was ruled from Bathgate Castle. Highlight in the history of the castle came in the early 14th century when King Robert the Bruce granted it to his daughter Princess Marjory when she married Walter his Lord High Steward, which led, of course, to the founding of Scotland's famous royal house of Stewart. Sadly Bathgate Castle has long since disappeared from its site to the south of the town, where the golf course is now situated, but it is still faithfully remembered by the town's coat of arms and by the local school children who every June on Procession Day, dress up as the royal couple and the lords and ladies of their court, thus reminding inhabitants of their town's historic origins.

Although later Scottish kings and queens and especially James IV and his young English bride Margaret Tudor are known to have hunted over Bathgate Moss, the town's royal connections, unlike those of its neighbour Linlithgow seven miles to the north, did nothing to help it grow and throughout the middle ages and for some time afterwards it remained a small village, whose only importance was as a stopping place between Scotland's lowland cities.

During these centuries Bathgate was in fact mainly overshadowed by the nearby village of Torphichen, where the powerful Knights of St. John built their Scottish headquarters and which was always the scene of much activity as the Order's tenants travelled from as near as Knights-ridge in Livingston and from as far north as Elgin to pay their ground rents. After the Reformation, however, the Knights were forced to leave Torphichen and in the end while it settled back to the slow pace of Scottish village life it was Bathgate which became a busy bustling burgh, for it was situated on top of a fortune in the shape of a rich coal deposit.

Unlike a similar coal field ten miles to the north at Bo'ness which was exploited as early as the 12th century, because it could be easily marketed by ships sailing in and out of the Firth of Forth, Bathgate's coal had to wait until the improvements in land transport during the late 18th century and the simultaneous growth in Scottish industry suddenly made it worth developing. At the same time Bathgate became a centre for the young but fast growing Scottish textile industry, a fact still recalled in the town by the retention of Weavers' Court as a local place name.

Then during the 1850's Bathgate received an even greater boost when Scottish industrialist, the development of the American oil industry. In his search for oil to meet the needs of Britain's ever expanding Victorian industrial empire, Young was sent some samples of coal from Bathgate's Boghead Pit. With them came a note saying that local miners called this type of coal 'parrot or cannel' coal, because when it burned it spluttered like a chattering parrot, while at the same time giving a light as bright as a candle. Young was intrigued and when he tested the samples proved they had a higher oil content than any other coal in Britain. Young then demonstrated his business acumen as well as his scientific skill by patenting the process and Bathgate's prosperity as the world's first oil boom town was ensured. Soon Young discovered that it was also possible to produce oil from the other local rock called shale and Bathgate again benefitted from the production of a wide range of by-products. Still more industries including iron and steel works flocked to the town to supply the needs of the collieries and shale mines, making Bathgate one of Scotland's best known industrial towns.

It is the prosperous, confident Bathgate of this period from around 1880 to 1931, which the postcards and pictures in this book recall, from the solid stone villas and long grey terraces, which the factory owners built, the first for themselves and their families, the latter for their workers, to the new churches where they worshipped together on Sabbath mornings and from the solid stone schools where their off-spring received an equally solid Scottish schooling to the 'shows' where they squandered their Saturday pennies at the end of each annual Procession Day.

Bathgate 'Bairns' still look back each Procession Day, but it takes a brave 'Bairn' to look forward at the present time, for the town has suffered a series of blows ranging from the failure of the giant Leyland Truck and Tractor Plant for which there were such high hopes when it was established in the 1960's to the shut down of the town's electronic industry and now in April 1985 the news of the closure of Polkemmet, the last pit in the whole area.

But Bathgate does have advantages including excellent transport connections, first rate education facilities from nursery schools to the West Lothian College of Further Education and good sports and leisure provision, especially its beautiful hinterland of the Bathgate Hills, where the 1,000 foot high Knock Hill actually belongs to the townsfolk. Thus, although Bathgate may never recapture the richness of its Victorian oil boom days, it will continue to be a place where families will choose to raise their children, content in the knowledge that its civic fathers will always strive to make it a place which lives up to its motto: 'Commune Bonum Intra Muros,' for the good of all who live within its boundaries.

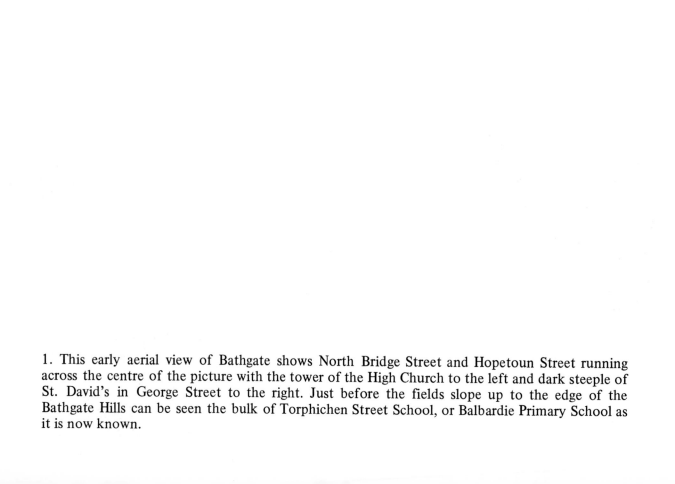

1. This early aerial view of Bathgate shows North Bridge Street and Hopetoun Street running across the centre of the picture with the tower of the High Church to the left and dark steeple of St. David's in George Street to the right. Just before the fields slope up to the edge of the Bathgate Hills can be seen the bulk of Torphichen Street School, or Balbardie Primary School as it is now known.

2. This picture of the oldest part of Bathgate was taken in 1884 shortly after the completion of the new High Church whose tower looms in the background. It shows Main Street and the house on the left hand side where Bathgate's most famous son, Sir James Young Simpson, pioneer of anaesthetic surgery, was born in 1812. Simpson lived here until he became a medical student at Edinburgh University at the age of only fourteen. He successfully completed his studies when still only eighteen and became a member of the Royal College of Surgeons, but was considered too young to be granted the degree of Doctor of Medicine, despite the fact that the year before he had saved the life of a patient. To fill in time Simpson tried to find a ship in Leith Docks to spend a year as ship's surgeon, but no vessel would sign him on because of his youth and his application to become surgeon in the village of Inverkip proved equally unsuccessful. Disappointed and short of money, Simpson moved in with one of his brothers, who had opened a bakery in Edinburgh and earned his keep by delivering bread, just as he had done in the days of his youth delivering the rolls from the family bakery in Bathgate. In 1832 life began to forge ahead again for the brilliant young Simpson when he obtained his degree and the post of assistant to the Professor of Pathology at Edinburgh, but he never forgot his West Lothian home town and on one of his visits to it in 1861 presented a silver thimble to be competed for annually by the girls of Bathgate Academy, 'in memory of his only sister Mary', who, he told the assembled pupils, following the death of his mother, had always faithfully and ungrumblingly darned his stockings.

3. The old town of Bathgate lingered on even after the proud new tower of the High Church was erected in 1884. Today, a century later, it has all but disappeared, but soon the town's first museum will help local people recall what life was like in their home town in days gone by. One feature of life even in those days was crime and the square building seen to the left of the picture was the town jail. While grown-ups were regularly jailed for a few days after appearing on Monday mornings at the Burgh Court on charges ranging from being drunk and disorderly to committing a public nuisance and from wife assault to petty theft, juvenile delinquents were punished with from three to twelve strokes of the birch rod for offences ranging from playing truant from school, to stealing coal from the railway sidings.

4. These old buildings in Jarvey Street with their bow front, fore stairs and pantiles were demolished to make way for the headquarters of Bathgate Co-operative Society including the Co-op's well-known Speyside Function Suite. Jarvey Street is believed to take its name from the Jarves, a French Hugenot family, who came to Scotland to escape religious persecution in their homeland. Some of the family farmed land around Torphichen, where the name still occurs, while others continued the craft of weaving, which they had brought with them from France and established their little home workshops in the old part of Bathgate, where as a result it is said that they gave their name to Jarvey Street.

5. The last of the Bathgate weavers, Nisbet Easton, poses by his hearth side for the photographer. The kettle on the hob is ready to make the tea, while the open book by his side is a reminder that while Bathgate's weavers worked with their hands, they had keen brains, which not only helped to create their intricate woven patterns, but which were also put to good use after the long day's work to participate in the town's famous Victorian Green Tree Debating Society and to write poetry.

One of their members, spinning wheel maker John Stark, or Starkie as he was known throughout the town, was such a Burns enthusiast, that every year on the poet's birthday, 25th January, he insisted on taking a holiday, decorating his home and holding open house. He decked his cottage from roof to floor with flags and holly and set up in front of it a large wooden model, which he had carved and painted, of Burns, dressed in grey, working at the plough. Inside he always arranged a display for his many visitors of curios, which he claimed bore a connection with the poet. They were very varied, ranging from some old thatch from Burns' cottage at Alloway and stones from the River Doon, to two of Poosie Nancie's jugs and even, so he maintained, some hairs from Meg's grey tail. One of his proudest possessions was a little prayer book, which he believed had once belonged to the church-goer who had inspired 'Holy Willie's Prayer'. Whether or not the people of Bathgate truly believed in all of Auld Starkie's Burns' relics, they always turned up at his home on 25th January to join in the festivities and see his giant haggis and Starkie, dressed in his Sunday best, proudly welcomed them all. Many of the local bairns had perhaps an ulterior motive in keeping in with Starkie, for as well as making spinning wheels, he also made spinning tops for the youngsters and his 'peeries' were prized possessions. It is interesting to wonder if the one in picture 37 was made by him. Starkie died aged 75 on 30th December 1881, thus robbing Bathgate of one of its most colourful characters.

6. The tower of the High Church looms over the Corn Exchange in Jarvey Street. The Corn Exchange provided the auction rooms where local farmers sold their crops, but after the sales were over its large hall often provided the setting for the town's dinners and dances and it is in this latter role that it survives to this day. Known for many years as the Palais, it occupies a fond place in the memories of many Bathgate couples who first met on its crowded dance floor. Today the style of dancing has changed and it has become the Queen's Disco, but it is still a popular meeting place for the town's young people.

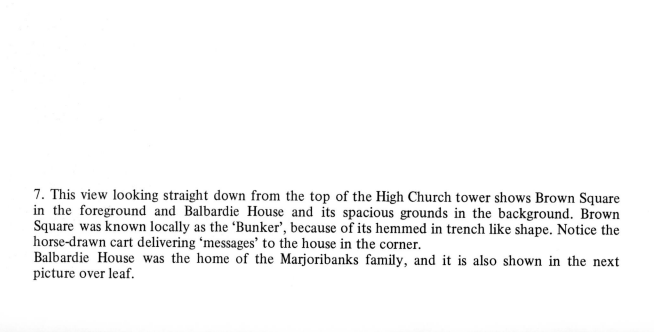

7. This view looking straight down from the top of the High Church tower shows Brown Square in the foreground and Balbardie House and its spacious grounds in the background. Brown Square was known locally as the 'Bunker', because of its hemmed in trench like shape. Notice the horse-drawn cart delivering 'messages' to the house in the corner.

Balbardie House was the home of the Marjoribanks family, and it is also shown in the next picture over leaf.

8. This is one of the few remaining pictures of Balbardie House, now long since demolished, although the name is still remembered in that of Balbardie Primary School, whose headmistress Mrs. Myra MacPherson does much to interest her young pupils in the history of the area.

Balbardie House as seen in this photograph was clearly an impressive mansion as befitted its builders and owners, Bathgate's best known family in Victorian times, the Marjoribanks, after whom Marjoribanks Street is named.

The Marjoribanks were always a very publicly minded family and it was one of their number Alexander Marjoribanks who as the town's first Provost in 1814 led the legal battle to ensure that Bathgate's benefactor John Newlands' intention in his will that his money should be used to build a 'school for the bairns of Bathgate' was honoured. Unfortunately the court proceedings and the time needed for interest to acrue on Newlands' capital meant that it was almost twenty years later in 1833 before the first classes were admitted to the new school and one boy who missed out on the added educational advantages which the new school offered was Bathgate's most famous son, Professor Sir James Young Simpson of chloroform fame.

However, when as a laddie young Simpson came each day to Balbardie House, to deliver morning rolls from his family's bakery in Main Street, Alexander Marjoribanks soon recognised how bright the wee delivery boy was and christened him 'The Young Philosopher', a nickname of which Simpson was always proud, along with the two others which he bore as a result of his Bathgate childhood. These were 'The Box o' Brains' as he was dubbed by his other customers amongst the townsfolk and 'The Wise Wean' as he was always referred to by his Bathgate schoolmaster, dominie Henderson, who himself bore the nickname of 'Timmerleg' because of his artificial limb, amputated sadly long before his cleverest pupil discovered the pain saving qualities of anaestetics.

9. The Balbardie House staff's summer outing was one of the highlights of the summer season. The large number of staff was in no way unusual for a Scottish mansion in the days when most young girls left school at the age of twelve to go straight into service first as kitchen, scullery and below stairs maids and then to work their way up to posts such as parlour maids and even cook. Here all the members of the household are obviously dressed in their 'Sunday best' clothes for this long looked forward to break from household routine. It is particularly interesting to note that with the exception of the young girl seated on the grass on the extreme left every person in the picture is wearing a hat, and her bonnet is lying by her side on the grass. The gentleman with his arm around her is John Addison senior and his son John Addison junior is standing behind him. Others whose names survive include Mrs. White, who holds her little daughter in her arms while her hand rests on the shoulder of her young son George. His brother Alexander is the boy with the white Eton collar sitting on the rug holding one of the footballs next to Miss Robertson and Miss Hastie. The White children's father stands behind Alex in the back row fourth from the right. As a result of the heat, jackets have been shed and lie draped over the bench seats of the horse-drawn brake, which at the end of this summer day of yester year would take them home to the big house and back to work until the excitement of another Balbardie House trip came around next year.

10. Bathgate's original High Church occupied the same site as the present building. Built in 1739 it was a very typical Scottish 18th century church, with the small belfry at the west end, the sole exterior adornment. Its stone walls were harled to protect them from the effects of weathering and it was roofed with slate. After serving its congregation for almost a century and a half it was demolished in 1883 to make way for the present much more elaborate Victorian church, whose impressive clock tower is seen in several of the pictures in this book. Built in Norman style it cost £8,000 to erect and its bell, which chimes every Sunday for morning worship, was donated by former Bathgate Provost John Waddell. When installed it was valued at £250. The church's fine pipe organ was installed in 1899.

11. This strangely shaped wooden bench can still be seen in Bathgate's High Church, but it is soon to find a place in the town's new museum. For this is the famous 'Cutty Stool' or Seat of Repentance and was used frequently as a means of punishment by the ruling body of the church, the Kirk Session, whose members in the past wielded vastly greater powers than they do today. From the time of the Reformation to the 19th century the elders of the Kirk Session met religiously every week to discipline the fellow members of their congregation and any who had dared to miss the Sunday service, or who had perhaps either spoken or worse still fallen asleep during the minister's lengthy sermon, could be duly punished by being made to sit in full public gaze directly below the pulpit on the Seat of Repentance.

To make absolutely certain that the wrong-doers were seen by all, the Seat of Repentance was raised above the height of the other pews and the miscreants were often made to wear white gowns. Other crimes punished by public exposure on the Seat of Repentance included swearing, quarrelling with neighbours and wife beating, but the most frowned upon was what the Session Clerk carefully noted down as 'fornication' and the most unusual feature of the Bathgate 'Cutty Stool' was that it had two seats so that both of the couple who had shared in this sin, could likewise share in their punishment together.

The most famous Scot to be publicly humiliated in this way for such behaviour was none other than the poet Robert Burns, but at least he got his own back by writing 'Holy Willie's Prayer'.

The Kirk Session also exercised discipline over all of the children of the parish. Erring bairns were not made to sit on either of the seats, but were instead made to bend right over the middle section so that their bottoms were well positioned for the Kirk Session's servant the Beadle to administer corporal punishment with the birch rod.

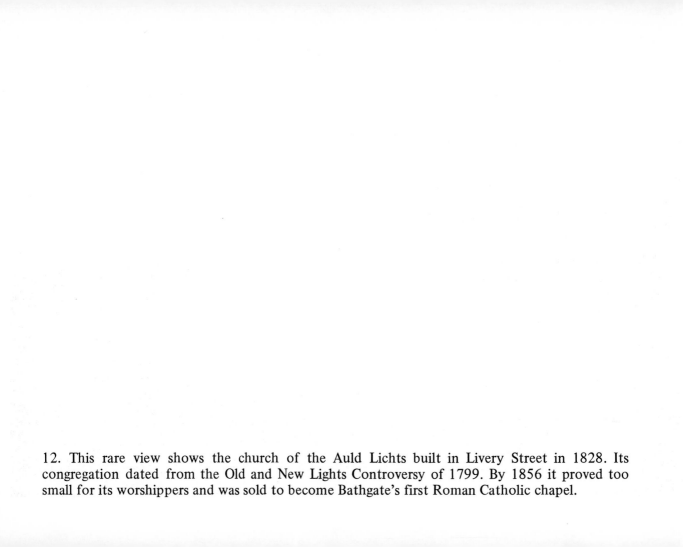

12. This rare view shows the church of the Auld Lichts built in Livery Street in 1828. Its congregation dated from the Old and New Lights Controversy of 1799. By 1856 it proved too small for its worshippers and was sold to become Bathgate's first Roman Catholic chapel.

13. During Victorian times, Bathgate's Roman Catholic population grew steadily until by the beginning of this century they had outgrown their original chapel in Livery Street and using the same site, the parishioners decided to build a fine new church. The laying of the foundation stone took place in 1908 and despite heavy rain a huge crowd waited to see it blessed by the Most Reverend James A. Smith, Archbishop of St. Andrews and Edinburgh.

Since then the Church of the Immaculate Conception as it was decided to call it has produced many well-known members of the Scottish clergy including Bishop James Monaghan and Bishop Vincent Logan of Dunkeld.

The church, which can seat 800, is one of the finest Roman Catholic churches in Scotland with particularly fine use of marble brought specially from Italy and Greece and including the magnificent high altar which is made of rich old Sienna marble.

A glimpse of the completed building with its unusual twin steeples can be seen in the background of picture 20.

14. The Steel Yard, or George Place, dominated by the impressive landmark of the steeple of the new St. David's Church, which was completed in 1906 and replaced the original St. David's, pictured opposite. The foundation stone of the new St. David's was laid in 1905 by Lord Roseberry. It was officially opened on Wednesday 25th April 1906 and was described as being of 13th century Gothic design. Stone from the original church was used in the building of the steeple, seen in this picture, which was described as being of plain construction from the base to the belfry, from which it flowered out to the top of the vane.

15. This Victorian view shows George Place or the Steel Yard, long before it was dominated by the steeple of the new St. David's Church, which was completed in 1906 and which can be seen in the previous picture. The Steel Yard is believed to have got its name not from the fact that steel was manufactured in Bathgate, but from the days when every Scottish town possessed its own set of measures and Bathgate's steel yard rod was imbedded in the street in this open space in the centre of the town for the use of local inhabitants.

Iron not steel was used to construct the gentlemen's convenience in the very centre of George Place as the Steel Yard was later rechristened and this rather French style urinal caused more controversy in Bathgate over the years than practically any other issue, until as late as the 1970's it was finally replaced by immaculately maintained public toilets in Mid Street. On either side of the controversial toilets can be seen South Bridge Street branching to the left and George Street, or Engine Street as it was known in these days, branching to the right with the Royal Hotel in-between.

The horse-drawn carriage crossing the entrance to South Bridge Street is crossing over into Whitburn Road.

16. This postcard shows the Royal Hotel in the Steel Yard or George Place as it was later called. Above the second storey bay window is printed the word 'Posting', which is a reminder of the days when mail coaches journeying between Edinburgh and Glasgow used to use it as one of their halts where horses could be changed and watered while passengers weary of the bumpy twelve hour journey between the two cities could snatch some food and fortify themselves for the remaining half of the trip with some suitable liquid refreshment. At this time the Royal was owned by Mr. W. White, whose name appears between the two single windows on the first floor. The buildings of the Royal Hotel still stand, but somewhat sadly they no longer offer any refreshments to modern travellers as they are now the offices of local solicitors Caesar and Howie.

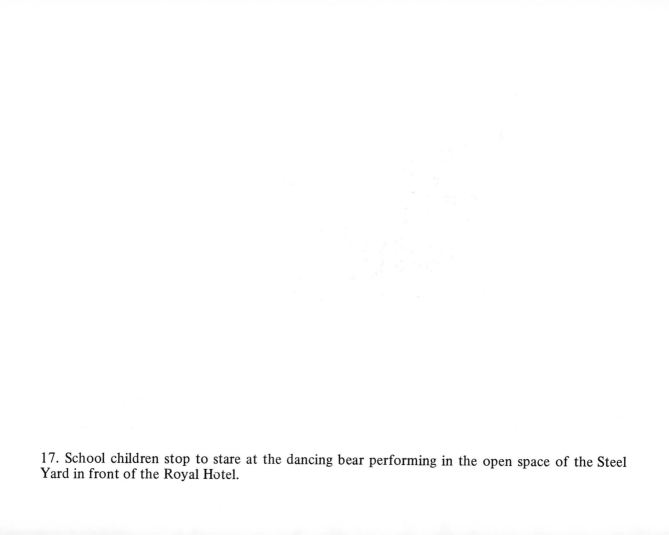

17. School children stop to stare at the dancing bear performing in the open space of the Steel Yard in front of the Royal Hotel.

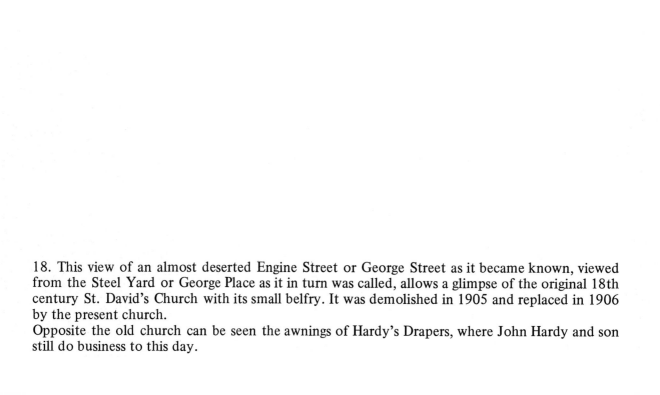

18. This view of an almost deserted Engine Street or George Street as it became known, viewed from the Steel Yard or George Place as it in turn was called, allows a glimpse of the original 18th century St. David's Church with its small belfry. It was demolished in 1905 and replaced in 1906 by the present church.

Opposite the old church can be seen the awnings of Hardy's Drapers, where John Hardy and son still do business to this day.

19. As boys play in the middle of the street it is difficult to imagine Engine Street as it is described in this postcard view of George Street as it is now known as Bathgate's main shopping street. At present it is being changed back to something like its former self as it is now being turned into a pedestrian only shopping precinct. This view looks north west up the street towards its junction with Hopetoun Street. The tree lined garden on the left beyond the old fashioned gas lamp, fronted the Georgian home of the local doctor. It was later demolished to make way for more shops.

Why Engine Street was called originally by this rather strange name is a subject of argument in the town, but the most likely reason is that a mine pumping engine to rid the workings of flood water, was situated at the top of the street. It is also suggested that the name of the street was later changed to George Street as this was considered more fitting and dignified for addresses in Bathgate's main street.

Bathgate

Engine Street

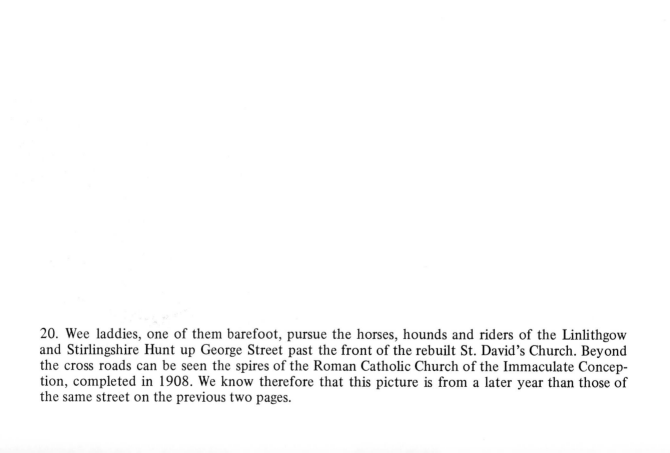

20. Wee laddies, one of them barefoot, pursue the horses, hounds and riders of the Linlithgow and Stirlingshire Hunt up George Street past the front of the rebuilt St. David's Church. Beyond the cross roads can be seen the spires of the Roman Catholic Church of the Immaculate Conception, completed in 1908. We know therefore that this picture is from a later year than those of the same street on the previous two pages.

21. Bathgate saddler William Brownlee shows one of his best customers, Sandy Stewart, proprietor of the Royal Hotel, a newly completed saddle. As the Royal had a flourishing livery stable attached to it, with an entrance to its courtyard directly opposite the saddlers where Greigs bakery is now situated in George Street, Mr. Brownlee received many orders from Mr. Stewart for both saddles and harness. Hanging on either side of the shop door are leather horse collars, which Mr. Brownlee had to tailor make for every individual order as every horse differed slightly. Fortunately Mr. Brownlee knew a lot about horses, because his father had farmed for many years in the Bathgate area, before giving up the land to try his hand as a business man in the town itself. At first the family opened a dairy in the oldest part of the town, probably in what is now known as Bennie's Yard, where the new Bathgate Museum is being created by school teacher Willie Millan. Then in 1858 old Mr. Brownlee saw the need for a saddlery in the town and opened the workshop in George Street from which he was soon supplying not only the local livery stables and farmers, but also as a side line the local teachers with the long lithe leather tawse, the supple, slashed, split thonged snake like straps with which they chastised their scholars in time honoured Scottish tradition. After over a century and a quarter in the saddlery trade, and in the same premises in George Street, Brownlees is now the oldest business in Bathgate, with its founder's great grandson Stewart still producing top quality leatherware, some of it for his own horses which his family keep at their home, Craigs Lodge, on the outskirts of Torphichen, Bathgate's neighbouring village.

22. The Linlithgow and Stirlingshire Hunt meets in Torphichen Square as it still does on occasion today.

In front of the white washed range of buildings notice the gentlemen who have travelled by horse-drawn brake to the village for the occasion. They have stopped in front of the village coffee shop, whose light can be seen above the door, but the start of the hunt was always marked by the handing round of a somewhat more potent stirrup cup, served from the Torphichen Inn, which under the direction of the Davidson family still does a thriving trade in meals and drinks to this day.

Notice the village children on the slope and the older youths in the middle of the Square, eyeing the horses and the top hatted, pink coated members of the hunt.

Today fox hunting is a much more controversial sport and meets are often interrupted by hunt saboteurs from the cities and Scottish universities, but it still has a great deal of support from local young people, who enjoy the thrill of riding their horses and ponies across the open countryside around the village, where many gymkanas and other riding events are also held.

23. Torphichen's oddly shaped village square remains largely unchanged today, but the peacefulness of this picture taken at the turn of the century is in marked contrast to the hustle and bustle of the traffic which now passes through the village.

One building which has disappeared is the old village hall, whose arched door can be seen in the centre of the picture. So too has the single storeyed cottage to the left of it, while the adjacent two storeyed building became the village's Co-operative Store and with much enlarged ground floor windows is now an antique store.

Today both of the village's shops are situated at either end of the attractive range of late 18th century buildings, seen behind the well erected to mark Queen Victoria's diamond jubilee in 1897. The village post office is now housed in the little single storeyed white washed cottage, while the house next door is now a private home, but was originally the village coffee shop, whose external lamp above the door was meant to attract travellers.

The open space in the foreground of the picture, where the little girls have spread their rugs ready for airing and beating, is now occupied by houses.

24. The High Brae, Torphichen, remains much the same today as it looked in this picture taken at the beginning of this century, except that the road has now been surfaced!

Notice the red pantiled roofs of the cottages on the left and the more typically Scottish grey slate roof of the late Georgian house in the centre. Its stone work has been left exposed, but that of its neighbours on either side has been harled. Harling was often used in Scotland to protect soft sandstone from wind and weather.

High Brae, Torphichen.

25. Slackend Cross Roads to the south of Torphichen on the road to Bathgate, is still easily recognisable, despite the new houses which have replaced the tree and the field.

Slackend House in the background, which belonged to Bathgate lawyer A.K. Fleming, now has a row of neighbours stretching up the hill to the left, but otherwise remains the same. The farm steading on the right later became a garage.

Slackend Farm to which the steading belonged is of particular interest as it at one time belonged to the Simpson family, whose grandson was Sir James Young Simpson, who gained fame as the Victorian doctor who pioneered the use of chloroform. During his childhood in Bathgate, young Simpson often walked out to spend the day on the farm and it is said that he delighted in listening to stories about earlier generations of his family at Slackend and in particular about their belief in superstition.

One story often told about the Simpsons was about the day a gypsy was turned away empty handed by one of the farm servant girls and as a result put a curse on its land. When farmer Simpson returned from work in the fields and heard of the curse, it is said that he dashed after the gypsy. He caught up with her in Torphichen Square and grasping hold of her pulled out his knife and scratched the sign of the cross on her forehead as the only way to lift her curse.

The story which scared young Simpson most was one about how his grandfather tried to rid his herd of disease, by digging a pit and then burying a healthy cow alive to try to appease the evil Lord of Murain, the wicked spirit of the land.

SLACKEND. TORPHICHEN.   R. BRAID. Photo.

26. Torphichen in the snow forms a charming Christmas card like scene. The little pantiled roofed cottages have long since disappeared, but the tall tower of the Knights of St. John's 12th century Preceptory and the adjoining 18th century parish church with its little belfry, still stand. Torphichen became the Scottish headquarters of the Order of St. John in 1168, when the Knights were granted these lands by the Scottish king. From here they administered all of their other possessions in Scotland as far north as Elgin and gathered their rents with which to finance their work on the Crusades or Wars of the Cross in the Holy Land, where to this day they maintain an eye infirmary in Jerusalem.

The Knights of St. John, who claim descent from their patron St. John the Baptist and who claim to be the oldest order of chivalry in the world, fulfilled a three fold religious, military and medical role, safeguarding the bodies and souls of pilgrims on the Crusades, and at Torphichen evidence of all three roles can still be found. The Preceptory at Torphichen is one of the few ecclesiastical buildings in Scotland with military architectural features, including battlements and a defensive staircase, while the whole site was formerly surrounded by a moat and battlements and the road in the picture is still called the Bowyett from the bow butts or archery targets where shooting was practised.

A reminder of the hospital which the Knights ran is provided by the leper squint, the small slanting window through which patients suffering from leprosy could look into the church and witness the service, without themselves being seen or coming into contact with other worshippers.

Finally the Preceptory, named after the Christian Precepts, or Choir as it is often called, because that is the part of the church still standing, is a reminder of the Knights' services, revived once each year on St. John's Sunday in June.

27. Torphichen's parish minister, the Reverend Mr. Beale, walks proudly beside the lead horse on this sunny summer Sunday School outing. All of the local farmers lent their horses and their large wheeled hay carts for this annual occasion, which always took place on a Saturday afternoon in June or early July.

The destination for this summer pilgrimage was often Caribber Glen to the north of the village where, after a picnic and races on the grassy slopes of the glen, the little girls in their white summer dresses could tuck their skirts and petticoats into their knickers and paddle in the cool waters of the River Avon.

The summer picnic marked the close of the Sunday School year and next day at the morning service in Torphichen Parish Kirk, many of the girls and boys would step forward to receive book prizes to mark perfect or excellent attendance, while their parents in their Sunday best looked on proudly.

Today Torphichen Kirk under its long serving minister, the Reverend Tom Crichton who has served the village for twenty years, still has a thriving Sunday School for local children and in addition holds special classes for them on Tuesday evenings.

28. Flat capped villagers pass the time of day and watch the photographer at work at the top of Torphichen's High Brae.

Torphichen has two braes, the High and the Low. The word brae is derived from Gaelic and means hill, which aptly describes these two roads which twist up from the village square to join Westfield Road at the point where this picture was taken.

The small cottages behind the iron railing have been replaced with modern ones and the one in the centre of the picture has been demolished and replaced by a two storey stone built villa.

St. John's Church, which can be seen in the background, still stands, but has been converted into the church hall, and has sadly been robbed of its little belfry and its weather cock.

HIGH BRCE or ST. JOHN'S CHURCH. TORPHICHEN.   A. BRCID. PhOtO.

29. St. John's United Free Church, Torphichen, was the first stone built Free Church built in Scotland, after the disruption of the Church of Scotland, in 1843.

As quarrels split the established church throughout the length and breadth of the land, half of the congregation left Torphichen Parish Kirk and built this small independent church on the hillside overlooking their former place of worship.

Its congregation stayed apart for over a century until in 1930 a well-loved parish minister, the Reverend Hugh P.R. MacKay was at last able to heal the breach and it was agreed that all of the villagers would once again worship together and that St. John's should become the church hall, a role which it still serves to this day, although the exterior has recently been altered.

The gateway to the left now leads to the Manse, a modern villa built to replace the parish minister's original residence, the much more interesting and historic Glebe House, which was sold by the Kirk Session and is now owned by the Wishart family. Glebe is the old Scottish word for the manse garden, which the parish minister was expected to cultivate to make up his meagre stipend or salary. Today the Wishart's use the Glebe to graze their horses, which are a popular sight when ridden through the village, bringing back memories of older, quieter times.

U. F. Church, Torphichen, near Armadale

30. Torphichen's biggest day of the year is still its annual Gala held on the third Saturday of June.

In this early picture, believed to have been taken in 1910, the village's school girl queen has just been crowned and parish minister the Reverend George Beale, who compered the proceedings, just as his successor the Reverend Tom Crichton still does to this day, is about to introduce the young maypole dancers.

Behind the platform the village well has been decorated, and although the coronation ceremony has now been moved from the Square to the more peaceful playground of the village school, it is at the old well that the young herald reads the proclamation announcing the crowning ceremony on the preceding Friday evening.

Across the road from the crowning ceremony, it is interesting to note that the McNair family in the one business combined hiring cabs and carriages with the sale of wines and spirits in their village grocery store, a combination, which in our 'don't drink and drive' days would no doubt prove more controversial. In the pre-First World War days pictured in this postcard, however, Scotland's roads were still peaceful enough to accommodate both the graceful open horse-drawn landau and the new fangled petrol driven motor car, which was soon to replace it.

McNair's shop, with the ground floor windows much enlarged, is now an antique store.

31. Torphichen Gala Day procession winds its way around the lawn in front of Wallhouse, whose large estate lies a short distance to the west of the village.

For over three centuries Wallhouse belonged to the same family, the Gillons, one of whose number, Henry, provided the £300 required in 1750 to build a new parish church for the village to replace that originally built by the Knights of St. John. Wallhouse is said to have had close connections with the Knights, because the name is claimed to be a corruption of Well House and a stained glass window in the staircase, depicts the members of the order coming to the well to draw water for use in the hospital and monastery which they established around the Preceptory, as their church in the village was known, from their acknowledgement of the Christian precepts. Another connection between Wallhouse and the Knights is the fact that the Gillon family's motto is 'Protection and Refuge', which is derived from the famous law of sanctuary, which the Order of St. John operated for one mile to the north, south, east and west of their headquarters, taking in the Wallhouse Estate. This law of sanctuary meant in the rough, tough times of the Scottish middle ages, when people were liable to take the law into their own hands, that any accused person able to reach these lands was assured of a fair trial.

Carved on the façade of the present house, shown in the picture, which was built in 1846, is the Gillon family coat of arms, whose ravens are a reminder that the name Torphichen is Gaelic for the hill of the ravens or magpies.

Wallhouse was for many years a local authority children's home, but as it is no longer needed for this purpose, now stands boarded up and deserted. Plans have however now been announced to re-open it as an old folks' home.

Wallhouse, Torphichen.

32. From the smallest baby, the children of Torphichen gathered on a gala day of days gone by to pose in front of the whitewashed cottage, which gained first prize as the best decorated house in the village, a competition, which is still held annually each June.

Most of the children are all dressed up for the big day, including three of the boys wearing white Eton collars, but notice the laddie in the middle, who despite the occasion still has bare feet. Notice too the boys' caps, the girls' buttoned boots and the white pantalettes of the little girl in the white sashed dress.

{ FIRST PRIZE } DECORATIONS

33. Proud villagers pose beneath their prize arch, built at the foot of the High Brae to mark Torphichen's gala day in the year 1910.
The single storey building immediately behind the arch has long since disappeared, but the houses on the brae itself still remain.

34. Boys enjoy a game of marbles in the playground of Torphichen Public School, which much modernised and enlarged, still serves the village today.

The school began in early Victorian days as a one room school. This first classroom still survives and houses the infant boys and girls, starting their education for the first time at the age of four and a half or five. Carved on the outside wall of this original classroom are two stone faces, which may represent Wisdom and Learning, while above the window is a representation of the old testament 'Burning Bush', the symbol of the Church of Scotland, which serves as a reminder of the church's important role in education during the 19th century, until in 1874 the government passed an Act of Parliament which was to make education at the primary stage compulsory and free.

This Act increased the number of children attending school and so in 1895 the one roomed school was extended to that seen in the picture.

PUBLIC SCHOOL, TORPHICHEN.

35. The raising of the school leaving age from 12 to 14 again necessitated another extension to Torphichen School as during the early years of this century it served both primary and secondary pupils.

Thanks to the large farming families living in the country area around Torphichen the school role at one time topped 200, until it was decided to transport the older boys and girls to schools in Bathgate.

For a time the primary role was kept high by the attendance of youngsters from Wallhouse Children's Home on the outskirts of the village and in 1958 West Lothian Education Authority modernised and extended the school, including the provision of a small assembly hall. During the 1960's a modern dining room complete with its own kitchen was also built in the school grounds. Since 1980, thanks to the closure of Wallhouse Children's Home and the smaller number of families with young children in the village, the number of children attending Torphichen School has fallen to 52, but such an important role does the school play in the life of the village that it is the fervent hope of all of the villagers that it will escape the education economy cuts, which have closed so many other small schools.

36. The Old School House, Torphichen, which is now the author's home. I first came to live in this large attractive old stone built school house in 1969, when I became headmaster of Torphichen School. I purchased the house upon Scottish local government re-organisation in 1975 and apart from the addition of a garage to the right hand gable wall and the creation of a curving entrance drive to the front, the house remains much as it looks in this picture.

In the dining room of the house I have gathered a small collection of items connected with the history of the school, ranging from the teacher's high desk and chair to heavy wooden Indian clubs used during Victorian times by the girls for gymnastic or drill lessons and from white China ink wells to the black leather tawse, or divided thonged punishment strap, which was every dominie or 'maister's' symbol of authority.

Longest serving dominie at Torphichen School was Andrew Elder, whose tombstone in the kirk yard states that he taught the village bairns for no less than forty years and other well remembered names amongst my predecessors include another Mr. Hendrie, who was no relation, a Mr. Menzies, Bob Currie O.B.E., who pioneered open plan education in West Lothian, and John McLellan, who has recently retired as head of another West Lothian school in the village of Stoneyburn.

When I was promoted to a larger school at Murrayfield in Blackburn on the opposite side of Bathgate in 1971, my successor was my infant mistress, Mrs. Mary Wilson, who became Torphichen Primary's first ever woman head. Mrs. Wilson, who lives in the village in the Kirkgate, along with her husband Ralph, who became well-known as head of the controversial Wester Hailes Community High School, has now served Torphichen Primary as its headmistress for 14 years. Now, in the summer of 1985, her husband has also returned to work in the area as Rector of Armadale Academy.

37. This next picture still has a schooldays theme, but moves back to Bathgate. Walking along the pavement in Mid Street this pupil from Mid Street Primary School, whose covered play sheds can be seen in the background, was pre-occupied with whipping his 'peerie' or little wooden spinning top, while behind him in the middle of the traffic free street two of the girls from the same school skipped happily on their way home from lessons.

It is interesting to note the boy's style of dress with his school cap perched on top of his 'pudding basin' hair cut, his collarless shirt, knee breeches, thick home knitted stockings and 'tackitty' boots. It is interesting also to notice that he carries his school books in a satchel worn at his side and not in a leather school bag worn on his back as became the fashion in later years.

38. Opened in 1833, Bathgate Academy was gifted to the town by its greatest benefactor, John Newlands. Newlands was brought up in Bathgate, but later emigrated to Jamaica, where he made his fortune as a plantation owner. He never returned to Scotland, but apparently never forgot his youth in West Lothian, because when he died in 1799, he left all of his considerable fortune to 'erect a free school in the parish of Bathgate'.

Unfortunately for Bathgate, Newlands' relatives were furious and disputed the will in a court battle which lasted fifteen years. In the end in 1814 the court ruled that only one fifth of Newlands' estate should be devoted to building the school, which he wanted 'for the bairns of Bathgate' and it took a further seventeen years for this sum of £14.500 to amass sufficient interest to allow work to start on the erection of the Academy 'on an open site to the south of the town'.

Two years later in 1833 the new school with its impressive neoclassical façade and its distinctive clock tower, was ready to admit its first pupils, but shortage of funds meant that they had to pay fees instead of receiving the free education which Newlands had wished and this continued to be the policy for the next half century.

The school opened with 400 boys and girls and only the Rector and three assistant masters to teach them, so it is hardly surprising that the trustees were so concerned about discipline that they decided that in addition to the terrors of thrashings with the traditional Scottish tawse, their Academy should have a scale of fines ranging from one half penny for any pupil jostling on the stairs to two pence for any child who dared climb out onto the roof.

Today Bathgate Academy is housed in modern buildings at Boghall, but the original building still serves an educational use as part of West Lothian College of Further Education.

Academy, Bathgate

39. Pupils of a previous generation listen intently to a speaker in the Academy Hall. The hall, with its tiered seats, was often the setting for the Oration Speech given each year on the Friday evening before John Newlands Day, by a distinguished former pupil of the school.

Many former pupils also have fond memories of crowding these same forms and bench seats to watch end of term concerts and productions of the Gilbert and Sullivan operas.

40. The John Newlands Memorial Choir photographed in 1910. John Newlands' link as founder and endower of Bathgate Academy is commemorated on one of the three banners behind the group and many of the members of the choir were teachers at the school, thus accounting for the other two banners honouring both teachers and trustees of the school.

The conductor of the choir seen standing holding his baton at the front of the choir on the right was popular academy music master Angelo Marsden and the gentleman standing on the side at the front was Mr. R.A. Robertson, Bathgate's provost from 1908 to 1914.

The photograph was taken by local photographer Mr. D. Aitken.

Over the years Bathgate has maintained its choral tradition with the North British Steel Foundry Choir staging regular concerts in the town at which well-known guest soloists have also been featured.

41. Bathgate Academy's most famous janitor Billy Spokes stands proudly on the steps of 'his' school on a sunny John Newlands Day morning. Before becoming the Academy's 'jannie' Mr. Spokes had served in the forces and he brought his military discipline into the playground where he was never afraid of enforcing it with the aid of his short swagger cane.

In addition to all of his caretaking duties, like many janitors in the years after the First World War, Mr. Spokes was also entrusted with teaching P.T. Officially these letters stood for Physical Training, but according to the Academy pupils under their 'jannie's' eagle eye they meant Physical Torture, as he drilled them in winter in the school hall and in summer in the sloping playground in front of the building.

Academy Rector Mr. Brown can be glimpsed walking out of the picture on the steps above the janitor.

42. Every school boy's dream came true in 1906 when fire swept through and gutted the north wing of Bathgate Academy. It is believed that the blaze started in one of the science laboratories and at its height, as flames leapt high in the sky, the entire roof crashed in.

The pupils who posed in the adjoining open field, while the photographer took this picture of the devastation, found their freedom short lived, however, for the Rector and his staff soon re-organised classes until the damaged classrooms could be rebuilt behind the Georgian façades.

43. The new fangled petrol driven motor fire appliance which was summoned all the way from Edinburgh, twenty miles away, to try to fight the Academy fire. Some local people somewhat unkindly maintained that the blaze was actually kept going until the city firemen arrived so that they could show off their new equipment, but they were too late to save the north wing of the school.

As some of the Academy's young pupils looked on fascinated by this latest wonder of the age, the helmeted firemen posed for the photographer in Marjoribanks Street to the south of the school, where West Lothian College of Further Education and the Telephone Exchange now stand.

44. Secondary education in Bathgate was completely reformed in the summer of 1931 with the opening of two enormous new twin schools on adjacent sites in Edinburgh Road.

This picture shows the newly erected Lindsay High School, named after the Reverend John Lindsay, minister for many years of St. John's Church, who was a prominent member of West Lothian Education Committee. The school was designed as a technical high school, as part of a tripartite system of education to serve not only Bathgate but also the surrounding towns. The idea of this system was that the academically brightest children from not only Bathgate but Armadale, Whitburn, Blackburn, Livingston, Stoneyburn, Longridge and Fauldhouse should all be educated together at Bathgate Academy, where they would receive a traditional classical education including Latin and Greek. The Lindsay High would then cater for boys and girls from all of these towns whom the famous 'Qualy' or Qualifying Examination had deemed would be more suited to a more practical secondary education with the emphasis on technical, scientific, commercial and domestic education, but with the expectation that the majority would go on to take their Scottish Higher Leaving Certificate. Those children not expected to succeed in secondary school examinations remained in the senior sections of their primary schools, which were later redesignated Junior Secondary Schools. It was this third strand to this secondary education system, which left a sense of stigma and which ultimately led to its abolition in 1968 and its replacement by the present comprehensive system. Until then, however, the Lindsay provided a very sound schooling for the pupils allocated to it and many were proud to wear its distinctive brown and gold uniform.

THE LINDSAY HIGH SCHOOL, BATHGATE   (11)

45. Immediately adjacent to the Lindsay High School stood its twin school, St. Mary's Academy. It was opened at the same time in 1931, when West Lothian Education Authority decided for the first time, as part of its secondary education reshuffle, to provide separate secondary schooling for all Roman Catholic pupils. Like the Lindsay St. Mary's catered not only for Bathgate children, but for the academically brightest Roman Catholic boys and girls from all the neighbouring towns and in its case it cast its educational net still further to take in pupils from as far away as Bo'ness, Linlithgow, Winchburgh, Kirkliston, Queensferry, Broxburn and Uphall. As well as providing for the religious needs of its 1,000 pupils, St. Mary's also ensured their sound secondary education, doing particularly well in commercial subjects, with several pupils winning top places in the Civil Service Examinations. With the opening of two new secondary schools and the emphasis thus being placed so visibly on religious differences, it might perhaps have been expected that there would have been aggravation between their pupils, but on the whole they existed happily side by side and with the exception of occasional winter snow balls fight pitched battles, reserved their joint rivalry for the pupils of Bathgate Academy. On the sports field the royal blue and gold colours of St. Mary's were often to the fore with the boys and girls urged on by their well-known sporting Rector, Canadian, Dr. McCabe, who himself had been an ice hockey star. In 1966 St. Mary's expanded to take in the Lindsay High School building, when the pupils of that school moved for the last two years of its existence before comprehensive re-organisation to new premises at Boghall, but now sadly St. Mary's too is threatened with closure to be replaced by a large new Roman Catholic secondary school in Livingston.

ST. MARY'S SECONDARY SCHOOL, BATHGATE

46. John Newlands Procession Day is always marked in Bathgate by the building of decorative arches, but none nowadays rival the elaborateness of those of former decades. This magnificent example with its proud lion rampants won first prize in 1920.

The date written on the back of the postcard by its sender of 21st April 1920 is of interest for two reasons. First it shows the speed with which postcards of topical events were produced and sold as this was purchased and sent less than a week after the event. Secondly it proves that Bathgate's Procession Day was not always held on the first Saturday in June as is now the case but appears to have been a moveable feast.

The message on the card reads: *Dear Sister, Just a few lines hoping it find you and Jim well as it leaves us the same except Jim he is of school with the mumps but he is now about alright again. I had Mother and Mrs. Rennie here on Friday. I think they enjoyed themselves. They got a nice day for the procession. There was a lot of people here. I was glad it kept fair because it was raining all week. I am expecting Beatie through on Saturday for the weekend. It is the holiday on Monday. There were a lot of dancers at the procession and Agnes told her Granny she wanted an umbrella to dance with. She was singing all the songs to her. This is two postcards of the arches. One shows the first prize one. Hoping to here from you soon again, good night, love from all to Jim and you from Jeanie.*

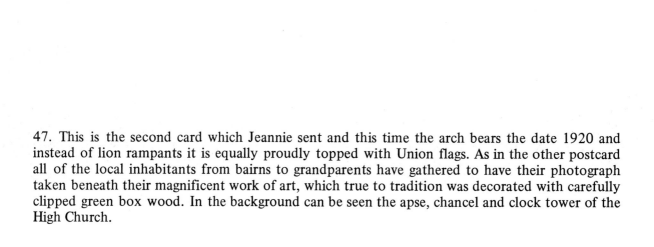

47. This is the second card which Jeannie sent and this time the arch bears the date 1920 and instead of lion rampants it is equally proudly topped with Union flags. As in the other postcard all of the local inhabitants from bairns to grandparents have gathered to have their photograph taken beneath their magnificent work of art, which true to tradition was decorated with carefully clipped green box wood. In the background can be seen the apse, chancel and clock tower of the High Church.

48. Bathgate's Procession Day was never complete without its fair or 'the shows' as the merry-go-rounds and side stalls were always known locally. This very early 'ride' appears to have been a version of the modern 'jungle ride', with full rigged sailing ships instead of the present day motor bikes to provide the thrills. It is interesting to note that a similar 'ride' with Viking boats, still draws the crowds at Copenhagen's famous Tivoli Gardens. Roberts famous livery stables, offering open carriages, small brakes and mourning coaches, can be seen in the background. Many of the carriages and brakes would no doubt have been in demand earlier in the day to take part in the Newlands Day procession through the streets of the town.

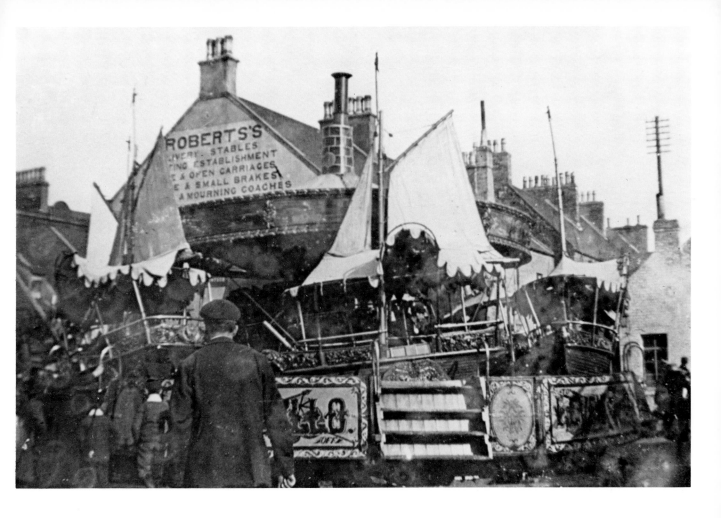

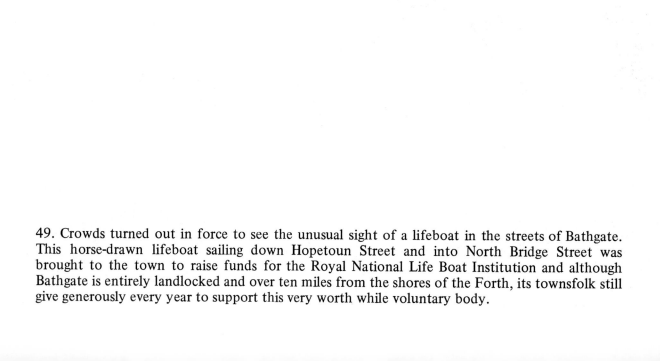

49. Crowds turned out in force to see the unusual sight of a lifeboat in the streets of Bathgate. This horse-drawn lifeboat sailing down Hopetoun Street and into North Bridge Street was brought to the town to raise funds for the Royal National Life Boat Institution and although Bathgate is entirely landlocked and over ten miles from the shores of the Forth, its townsfolk still give generously every year to support this very worth while voluntary body.

50. Girls push a pram as ladies enjoy a stroll on a sunny summer day in Cochrane Street. The single storey cottages, typical of Bathgate in Victorian times, were gradually giving way to the two storeyed stone built type of house seen on the corner. The old white washed building on the opposite side of the street was a dairy.

COCHRANE STREET, BATHGATE.

51. Crowds turned out in force in 1923 when subsidence in Bathgate's underground coal mine workings caused Hopetoun Street to be cordoned off and local residents to be hurriedly ordered to evacuate their homes. To add further to the excitement the cave-in caused a gas main to fracture and there was the added fear of an explosion as James Carlaw loaded his belongings onto the back of this open lorry. On this occasion the collapse of the old colliery workings caused no further damage and Mr. Carlaw and his neighbours were eventually able to return to their houses, but fifty years later in the 1970's further subsidence further up the hill resulted in several buildings being demolished and even more recently the town's new public library has been threatened by the sinking of more of these workings which run like a honeycomb below the streets of the town.

52. Samuel's barbers pole juts out into North Bridge Street looking up the hill towards Hopetoun Street. The red and white markings on the pole are a reminder of the days when barbers were barber surgeons and were often called upon to perform blood letting, thus the red for the blood and the white for the bandages to stem the flow when it was considered that the patient had been relieved of enough blood to cure them. The gold tip to the pole represented the gold bowl or basin in which the blood was caught and thus completes the traditional sign for the barber. Patients too squeemish to have blood letting performed by having their wrist slashed could choose to have the blood removed by black leeches which were stuck to their fore arms. By the time this picture was taken, however, Bathgate's barbers stuck strictly to shaving and giving short back and sides hair cuts.

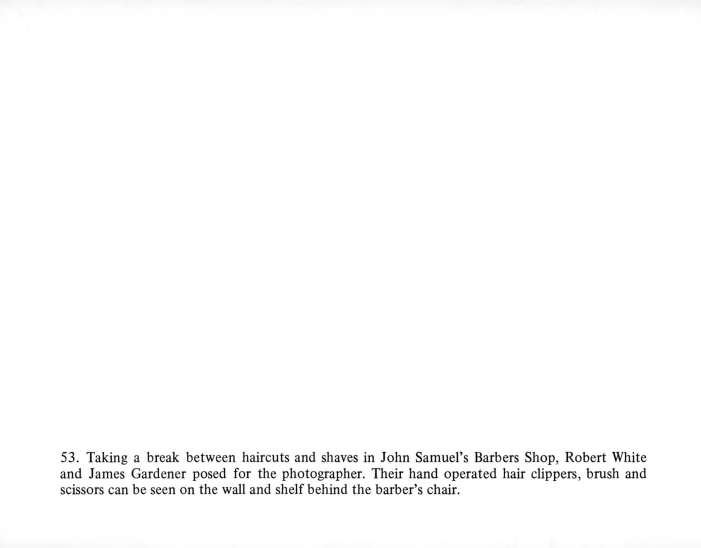

53. Taking a break between haircuts and shaves in John Samuel's Barbers Shop, Robert White and James Gardener posed for the photographer. Their hand operated hair clippers, brush and scissors can be seen on the wall and shelf behind the barber's chair.

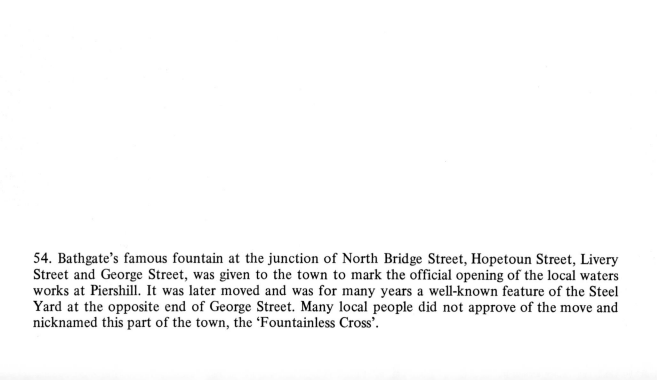

54. Bathgate's famous fountain at the junction of North Bridge Street, Hopetoun Street, Livery Street and George Street, was given to the town to mark the official opening of the local waters works at Piershill. It was later moved and was for many years a well-known feature of the Steel Yard at the opposite end of George Street. Many local people did not approve of the move and nicknamed this part of the town, the 'Fountainless Cross'.

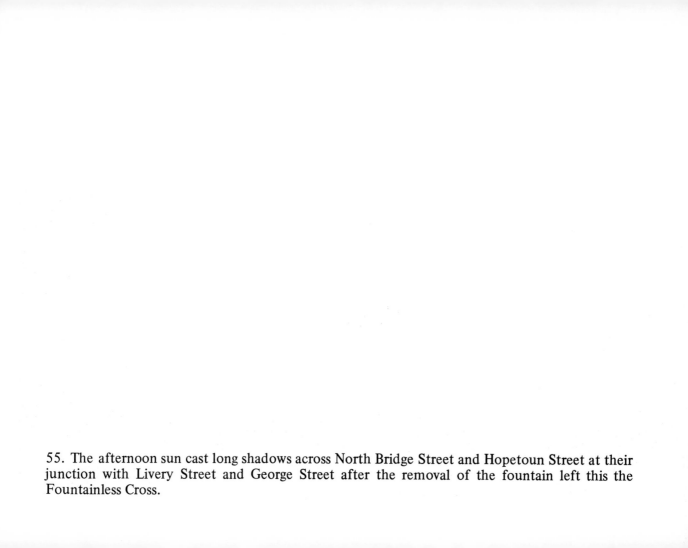

55. The afternoon sun cast long shadows across North Bridge Street and Hopetoun Street at their junction with Livery Street and George Street after the removal of the fountain left this the Fountainless Cross.

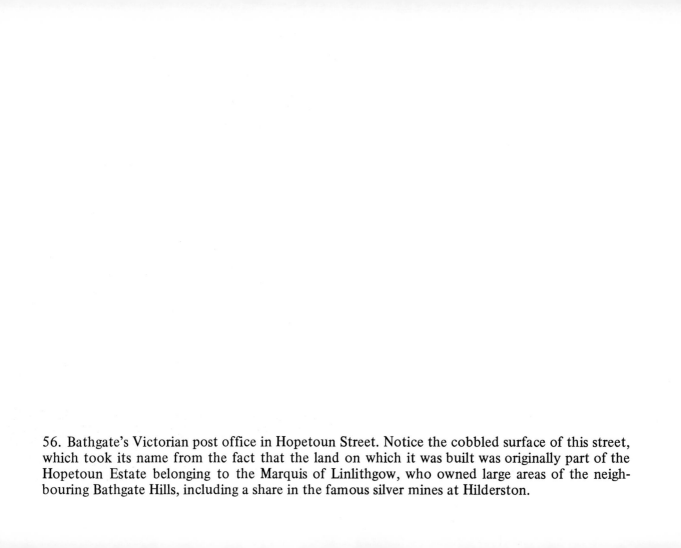

56. Bathgate's Victorian post office in Hopetoun Street. Notice the cobbled surface of this street, which took its name from the fact that the land on which it was built was originally part of the Hopetoun Estate belonging to the Marquis of Linlithgow, who owned large areas of the neighbouring Bathgate Hills, including a share in the famous silver mines at Hilderston.

57. All present and correct, the staff of Bathgate Post Office line up in front of their Victorian premises in Hopetoun Street just down the hill from where the public library is now situated. The size of the staff is a clear indication of the importance of the service which the Post Office provided in the days before telephones became common. A letter posted in Bathgate before breakfast would be delivered to any local address before lunch and with regular afternoon deliveries, townsfolk often used to send postcards to tell friends that they would call to visit them that evening, with a guarantee that they would thus be expected. For even speedier service the four smartly uniformed telegram boys were always ready to jump on their bicycles to rush news of important happenings sich as 'Matches, Hatches and Despatches', 'Marriages, Births and Deaths' to any part of the town or the surrounding outlying villages such as Blackburn, Seafield and Torphichen. The Post Office later moved to larger, more central premises in George Place, before moving to its purpose built modern sorting office in North Bridge Street, where it continues to serve the town as it has done since first established in 1840.

Today its services are different with telegrams a thing of the past and telephones entrusted to a separate organisation, but the Post Office is still crowded every weekday with townsfolk not only posting mail, but buying licences for everything from cars to television sets and even dogs and from collecting pensions and allowances to using its Giro Banking Service.

The best known public face of the Post Office is, however, still its uniformed postmen and now postwomen doing their daily rounds and many are as well-known today as the famous Robert Heigh, the 'postie' standing to the right of the telegram boys in the picture, was in his day.

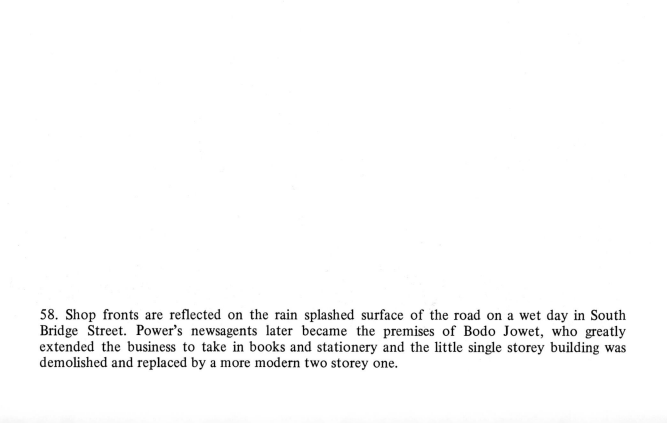

58. Shop fronts are reflected on the rain splashed surface of the road on a wet day in South Bridge Street. Power's newsagents later became the premises of Bodo Jowet, who greatly extended the business to take in books and stationery and the little single storey building was demolished and replaced by a more modern two storey one.

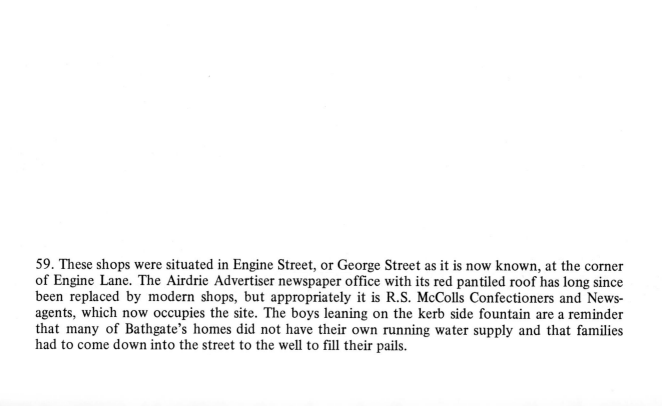

59. These shops were situated in Engine Street, or George Street as it is now known, at the corner of Engine Lane. The Airdrie Advertiser newspaper office with its red pantiled roof has long since been replaced by modern shops, but appropriately it is R.S. McColls Confectioners and News-agents, which now occupies the site. The boys leaning on the kerb side fountain are a reminder that many of Bathgate's homes did not have their own running water supply and that families had to come down into the street to the well to fill their pails.

60. Shop assistants with their white aprons pose outside the original premises of Bathgate Co-operative Society, which several years ago merged to become part of the giant Scot Mid Co-operative. Signs above the doors indicate the various services which the Co-op originally offered its members in Bathgate and they included boot and shoe making, baking and clothes from the drapers. The Co-op always delivered milk and rolls to homes throughout the town every morning and the stables where the horses and carts were kept were through the arched doorway. Every family had their own Co-op number and a 'check' book so that at the end of each quarter they could look forward to receiving a share of the profits which was always referred to as 'the divi' or the dividend and which was sometimes as high as thirty pence in the pound, a bounty which made it well worth while joining the Co-op and patronising its many shops and services.

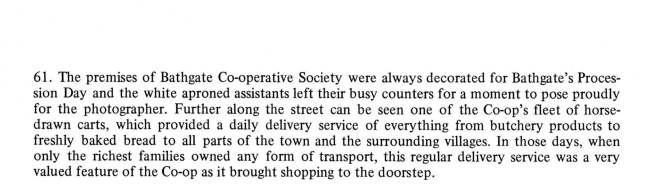

61. The premises of Bathgate Co-operative Society were always decorated for Bathgate's Procession Day and the white aproned assistants left their busy counters for a moment to pose proudly for the photographer. Further along the street can be seen one of the Co-op's fleet of horse-drawn carts, which provided a daily delivery service of everything from butchery products to freshly baked bread to all parts of the town and the surrounding villages. In those days, when only the richest families owned any form of transport, this regular delivery service was a very valued feature of the Co-op as it brought shopping to the doorstep.

62. This picture of Bathgate Chemical Works is a last reminder of the fact that the town was the site of the country's earliest oil refinery established by James 'Paraffin' Young on this site in 1848. It was Young who discovered how to extract oil, at first from coal and shortly afterwards from shale and the refinery was established to process coal from Boghead Pit from which the inventor obtained his first supplies. Soon afterwards Young was taken to the Court of Session in Edinburgh by Mr. Gillespie, the Bathgate landowner who had leased him the mineral rights and who was furious to find that instead of selling coal as he had expected, Young was making a great deal more money by producing oil. Young won the case and carefully protected his oil producing process with a patent which protected him and kept out the new found Texas oil until 1864. By then Young's experiments at Bathgate allowed him to diversify into many other oil related products, the most famous of which was paraffin, which provided safe fuel for lamps and which earned him his famous nickname.

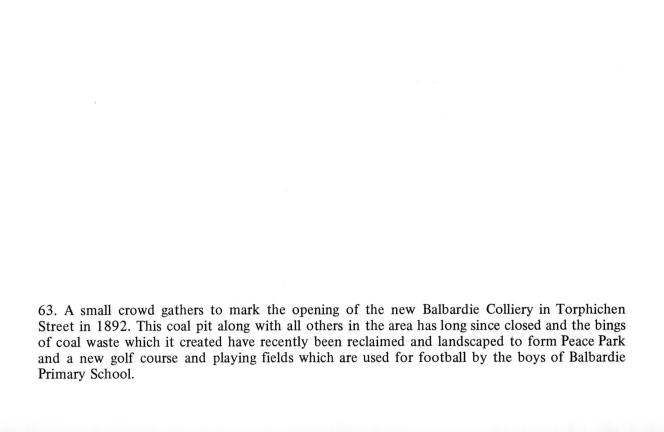

63. A small crowd gathers to mark the opening of the new Balbardie Colliery in Torphichen Street in 1892. This coal pit along with all others in the area has long since closed and the bings of coal waste which it created have recently been reclaimed and landscaped to form Peace Park and a new golf course and playing fields which are used for football by the boys of Balbardie Primary School.

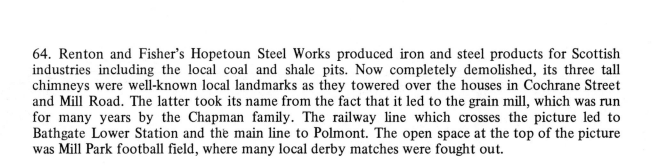

64. Renton and Fisher's Hopetoun Steel Works produced iron and steel products for Scottish industries including the local coal and shale pits. Now completely demolished, its three tall chimneys were well-known local landmarks as they towered over the houses in Cochrane Street and Mill Road. The latter took its name from the fact that it led to the grain mill, which was run for many years by the Chapman family. The railway line which crosses the picture led to Bathgate Lower Station and the main line to Polmont. The open space at the top of the picture was Mill Park football field, where many local derby matches were fought out.

65. Barrels of whisky form an appropriate background for this picture of the workforce at MacNab's Glenmavis Distillery, which was situated on the road to Torphichen to the north of the town. The distillery closed down during the late 1950's and its site is now occupied by a large garage, car show room and filling station, so it is particularly interesting to note the two horse power on which the whisky makers depended. What connection the pig held by the worker in the front row had with the distillery is a mystery and another puzzle is the inclusion of the postman who is seen standing in front of the left hand horse. It is interesting also to note the MacNab thistle trade mark painted on the wall beneath the pantiled roof.

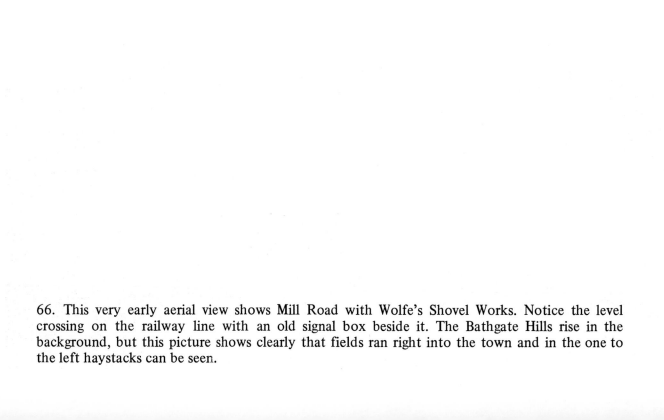

66. This very early aerial view shows Mill Road with Wolfe's Shovel Works. Notice the level crossing on the railway line with an old signal box beside it. The Bathgate Hills rise in the background, but this picture shows clearly that fields ran right into the town and in the one to the left haystacks can be seen.

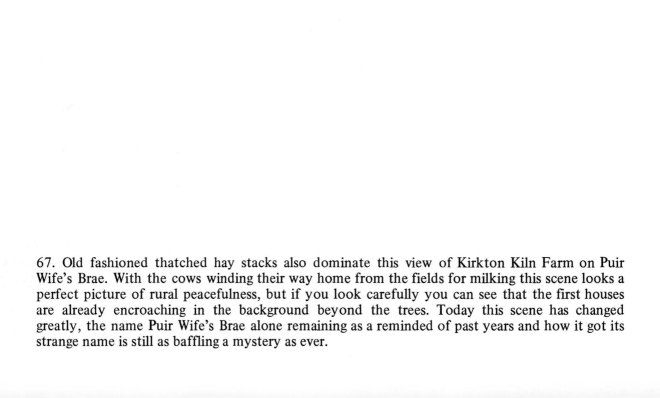

67. Old fashioned thatched hay stacks also dominate this view of Kirkton Kiln Farm on Puir Wife's Brae. With the cows winding their way home from the fields for milking this scene looks a perfect picture of rural peacefulness, but if you look carefully you can see that the first houses are already encroaching in the background beyond the trees. Today this scene has changed greatly, the name Puir Wife's Brae alone remaining as a reminded of past years and how it got its strange name is still as baffling a mystery as ever.

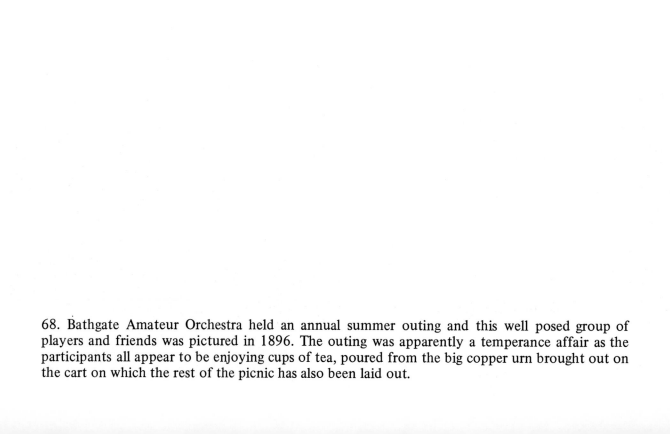

68. Bathgate Amateur Orchestra held an annual summer outing and this well posed group of players and friends was pictured in 1896. The outing was apparently a temperance affair as the participants all appear to be enjoying cups of tea, poured from the big copper urn brought out on the cart on which the rest of the picnic has also been laid out.

69. Driver and conductor pose proudly in front of the latest 1920's style omnibus. The bus was owned by the S.M.T., whose initials, which can just be seen on the dark band round the vehicle, stood for Scottish Motor Traction Company. Today the firm, which has been nationalised, is officially known as the Eastern Scottish division of Scottish Omnibuses, but local people still persistently refer to S.M.T. buses, proving that affection established over sixty years of excellent service is worth more than any amount of modern publicity.

Sadly there are no longer any conductors to pass the time of day with on the company's modern fleet of vehicles as they are now all one man operated.

70. A train approaches the platform at Upper Bathgate Railway Station. After a quarter of a century without a rail service, pressure from local residents has forced British Rail to agree to re-introduce trains between Bathgate and Edinburgh. Sadly the line in the opposite direction to Airdrie and Glasgow has been removed to make way for the new M8, M9 motorway link road, so restoration of this service seems unlikely. The re-opening of the Bathgate-Edinburgh line will however revive many memories among older local inhabitants of just how important the town's network of rail services used to be with passenger trains plying daily from the town's two stations, not only to Edinburgh and Glasgow, but to Linlithgow, Bo'ness, Falkirk and Polmont via Manual Junction, while children in Fauldhouse used to travel by train every weekday morning and afternoon to attend Bathgate Academy.

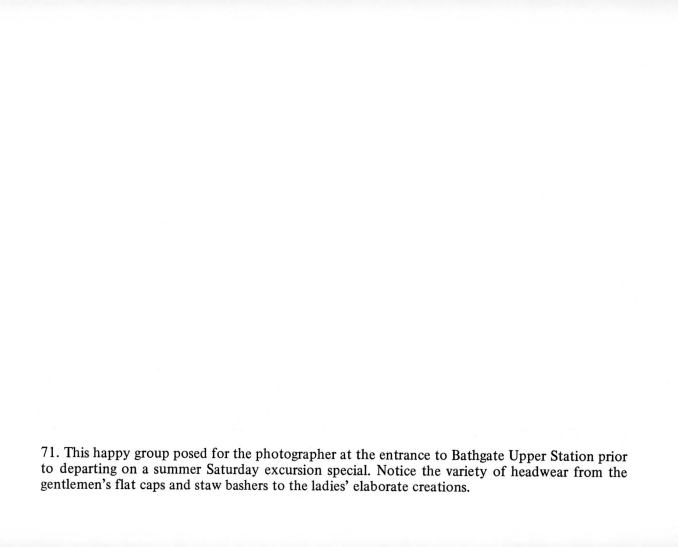

71. This happy group posed for the photographer at the entrance to Bathgate Upper Station prior to departing on a summer Saturday excursion special. Notice the variety of headwear from the gentlemen's flat caps and staw bashers to the ladies' elaborate creations.

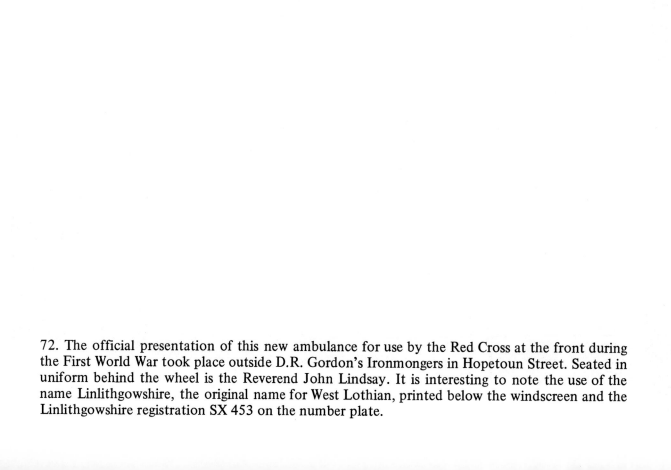

72. The official presentation of this new ambulance for use by the Red Cross at the front during the First World War took place outside D.R. Gordon's Ironmongers in Hopetoun Street. Seated in uniform behind the wheel is the Reverend John Lindsay. It is interesting to note the use of the name Linlithgowshire, the original name for West Lothian, printed below the windscreen and the Linlithgowshire registration SX 453 on the number plate.

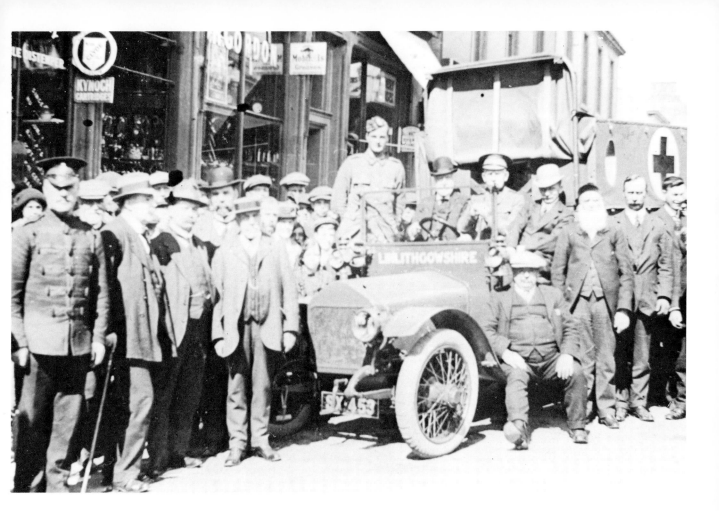

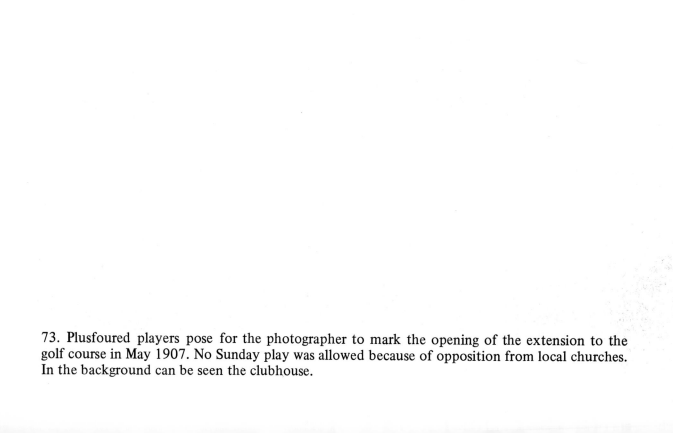

73. Plusfoured players pose for the photographer to mark the opening of the extension to the golf course in May 1907. No Sunday play was allowed because of opposition from local churches. In the background can be seen the clubhouse.

74. This postcard shows the Gothic Gates at the entrance to Kirkton Estate on the east side of the town. The estate was acquired many years ago by the town and is now a spacious public park whose many attractions include tennis courts, bowling green, paddling pool, children's playground and open air bandstand. The hillside seen through the arch is now built up with the many houses of Boghall and Limefield housing schemes and the premises of Bathgate Academy, Boghall Primary and St. Columba's School and Church all occupying this former open site to the east of the town. Opposite the Gothic Gates, the ruins of Bathgate's oldest church, from which the Kirkton estate took its name can still be seen and in the kirkyard lies the grave of Bathgate's martyred Covenanter, who was killed by the government dragoons in a running skirmish on the outskirts of the town.

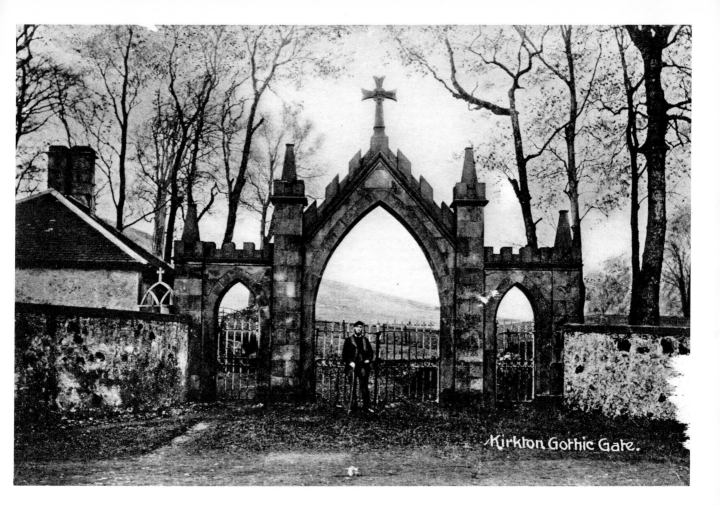

Kirkton Gothic Gate.

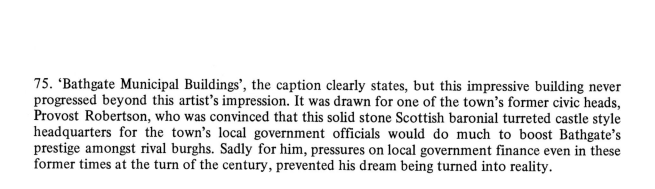

75. 'Bathgate Municipal Buildings', the caption clearly states, but this impressive building never progressed beyond this artist's impression. It was drawn for one of the town's former civic heads, Provost Robertson, who was convinced that this solid stone Scottish baronial turreted castle style headquarters for the town's local government officials would do much to boost Bathgate's prestige amongst rival burghs. Sadly for him, pressures on local government finance even in these former times at the turn of the century, prevented his dream being turned into reality.

BATHGATE MUNICIPAL BUILDINGS

76. Bathgate's official lamp lighter or 'leerie' James Cribben tends one of his lamps in Jarvey Street and recalls Robert Louis Stevenson's famous poem first published in 1885 in 'A Child's Garden of Verses' about his Edinburgh counterpart, 'The Lamplighter'.

My tea is nearly ready and the sun has left the sky.
It's time to take the window to see Leerie going by.
For every night at tea-time and before you take your seat,
With lantern and with ladder he comes posting up the street.
Now Tom would be a driver and Maria go to sea,
And my papa's a banker and as rich as he can be.
But I, when I am stronger and can choose what I'm to do,
O Leerie, I'll go round at night and light the lamps with you!
For we are very lucky, with a lamp before the door,
And Leerie stops to light it as he lights so many more.
And O! before you hurry by with ladder and with light,
O Leerie, see a little child and nod to him tonight!